A Machine Like Human

An inside narrative of the upgraded version of a new released writing AI, its massive advantages and the possible threat it poses to the world

```
Saraline Tusks
```

Copyright © 2024 by Saraline Tusks

All rights reserved. No part of this publication may be reproduced, distributed, or transmitted in any form or by any means, including photocopying, recording, or other electronic or mechanical methods, without the prior written permission of the publisher, except in the case of brief quotations embodied in critical reviews and certain other noncommercial uses permitted by copyright law

Table of Contents

Introduction..6
   Goal and Extent of the Book..8
Chapter 1: The Evolution of ChatGPT.............................. 10
   A Synopsis of AI Model History... 10
   Most Important Developments That Led to the o1 Series' Creation.. 13
   Discernments Between the New o1 Model and Early Models.. 14
   Impact on Handling Difficult Mathematical and Scientific Problems... 19
Chapter 2: The Capabilities of o1 – A Game Changer...... 22
   Intricate Reasoning and Solving of Problems...................... 22
   Practical Uses: Cancer Research, Quantum Optics, and Other Areas...24
   The Function of AI in Research and Healthcare.................27
   Applications of AI in Healthcare Research: Real-World Case Studies...29
   The Function of the o1 Model in Producing Coding Solutions and Complex Mathematical Formulas..................32
Chapter 3: Powering the AI – Energy Demands and Environmental Costs... 35
   The Unexpected Costs of AI's "Thinking".............................35
   Harmonizing Sustainability and Innovation........................39
   Government Policies and Business Reactions to Advanced

AI's Energy Requirements..42

Chapter 4: The Advantages of Human-like AI...................45

    Transforming Sectors: Education, Healthcare, and Other....45

    Enhancing Intelligence in Humans..49

Chapter 5: The Ethical Dilemma – A Machine That Thinks. 53

    Human-Like AI's Ethical Implications.....................................53

    AI's Effect on Employment and Society..................................57

    The Dangers of AI Strengthening Social Inequalities and Preserving Biases...61

    Apprehensions Regarding AI's Use in Collecting and Abusing Personal Data...63

    Talks Regarding How AI Should Be Managed and Regulated to Guarantee Safe Use..66

Chapter 6: The Potential Threat – Could o1 Outthink Humanity?...69

    Superintelligence: A Fear..69

    Who Should Oversee the Creation and Application of Such Potent AI?..73

    The Dangers of Using Cutting-Edge AI for Military Uses...76

Chapter 7: In Search of Balance – Integrating AI into Society Responsibly...80

    A Novel Collaboration: AI and Humans...............................80

    How Education Systems Must Change to Readiness Future Generations for an AI-Powered World...................................83

    Policy Changes Needed to Effectively Regulate and Manage AI on a Global Level...85

Chapter 8: The Future of AI – What Comes After o1?..... 88
    OpenAI's Future Prospects..88
    Theories Regarding AI's Potential to Address the Biggest
    Issues Facing Humanity... 92
    The Way Ahead: Prospects and Dangers................................ 95

Conclusion: A Machine Like Human – Friend or Foe?...... 99
    Human-Machine Collaboration's Future........................... 102

Introduction

Over the previous ten years, artificial intelligence has advanced significantly, but the introduction of OpenAI's new "o1" model represents a major turning point in the field's evolution. Up till now, ChatGPT and similar models have mainly been utilized for conversational and natural language processing jobs; they are quite good at producing text, giving information, and even helping with creative initiatives. But after the release of OpenAI's "o1" model, the emphasis has switched to more sophisticated reasoning and problem-solving skills, allowing AI to function at a higher cognitive level.

Beyond simply improving communication, the "o1" series aims to augment human-like thinking and provide previously unheard-of processing power to domains like advanced mathematics, physics, and healthcare. The o1 model marks a turning point in AI's capacity to reason—or, more precisely, think—through complex problems requiring in-depth analysis and multiple steps of reasoning. A major change from earlier iterations, OpenAI built this model to take more time "thinking" through queries before offering responses. More than ever, o1's capacity to improve upon its methodology, identify errors, and weigh many approaches to an issue brings it closer to human-like cognitive functions. The efficacy of this methodology in helping to annotate large, intricate datasets for biological research and solve challenging mathematical issues for quantum optics is already being evaluated.

One cannot stress the importance of this development enough. It poses concerns about the place of AI in human civilization in addition to creating new opportunities in domains requiring sophisticated cognitive processing. The o1 model marks a turning moment in the increasing integration of AI into daily life, bringing both possible threats and enormous benefits. This book addresses the ethical, societal, and environmental issues this new AI paradigm raises while examining its many benefits.

Goal and Extent of the Book

This book aims to provide readers a behind-the-scenes peek at the possibilities of the improved o1 AI model. We will follow the path that led to the creation of a computer that can "think" a lot like a person by looking into ChatGPT's past and development. The book will discuss the scientific and technological developments that enabled this breakthrough and show how artificial intelligence (AI) can transform fields like science, healthcare, and education. This, however, is not merely a jubilant narrative of AI's advancement.

The book will also critically look at the risks and difficulties that come with these developments. These include the loss of jobs, privacy issues, and the environmental impact of high-energy AI models. We want to give the reader a fair picture of AI's potential as well as its risks by examining its ethical ramifications and societal effects. Readers will acquire a deeper knowledge of what it means to live in a time when machines are starting to think, as well as what that could mean for humanity's future, throughout this voyage. In the upcoming chapters, we'll examine the inner workings of OpenAI's o1 model, weigh its advantages and disadvantages, and talk about the moral and societal obligations that accompany this innovative technology.

Chapter 1: The Evolution of ChatGPT

A Synopsis of AI Model History

From ChatGPT to o1 Since its conception, artificial intelligence (AI) has advanced significantly, and ChatGPT has played a key role in this development, particularly in the area of natural language processing. The creation of large language models (LLMs), notably OpenAI's ground-breaking GPT series, is where ChatGPT got its start. 2018 saw the release of the first GPT (Generative Pre-trained Transformer) model, which used a vast quantity of textual data to produce replies that resembled those of a human depending on the context. This model served as the foundation for one of the world's most sophisticated conversational AIs. In 2020, ChatGPT made its debut, utilizing the ground-breaking GPT-3 architecture at the time.

With 175 billion parameters, GPT-3 was able to generate responses that were more intelligent, cognizant of context, and cohesive than those of its predecessors. It might be able to comprehend instructions, produce original writing, condense data, and even help with code production. Though with some restrictions, GPT-3 and consequently ChatGPT were intended to react to user inputs in a conversational manner that resembled human interaction. ChatGPT is a tool that millions of people use worldwide, ranging from casual users to specialists in many industries, thanks to its capacity to hold discussions, facilitate content production, and carry out a broad range of cognitive tasks.

Even with these improvements, ChatGPT's depth of reasoning and multi-step problem-solving capabilities remained constrained in its early versions. Although the model was good at creating words, it frequently had trouble with intricate reasoning tasks. It could provide the impression of knowing without actually comprehending the topic's more profound ramifications. Furthermore, the system occasionally produced inaccurate or deceptive results, especially when posed challenging technical or scientific queries. OpenAI kept improving its models after realizing these drawbacks, which produced important advances.

As methods such as "fine-tuning" and "reinforcement learning with human feedback" (RLHF) were developed, the model's capacity to manage increasingly complex and varied questions was enhanced. The model's fine-tuning made it more task-specific, and the human-guided feedback loops provided by RLHF improved the model's decision-making process. These developments prepared the way for the o1 series, the next phase of development.

Most Important Developments That Led to the o1 Series' Creation

Comparing the o1 model to its predecessors, a significant advancement is evident. A major innovation that contributed to the development of the o1 model was the move away from statistical language generation and toward more sophisticated thinking abilities. The o1 model was created to take more time to process and consider issues before reacting, in contrast to earlier models that concentrated on producing text based on patterns in data. This made it capable of handling increasingly difficult jobs, such deciphering complicated mathematical puzzles or examining scientific data.

An additional significant development was the enhancement of multi-step reasoning. OpenAI came to the conclusion that in order for AI to be truly helpful in domains like physics or healthcare, it must be able to deconstruct complex issues into smaller, more manageable pieces, much like a human would. This capability is built into the o1 model, which enables it to perform more complex, multi-layered jobs with more accuracy and sophistication.

Discernments Between the New o1 Model and Early Models

The thinking abilities of the new o1 model are one of the biggest distinctions from previous models such as GPT-3. Previous models were frequently constrained by their incapacity to engage in actual critical thinking, despite the fact that they might generate remarkable results based on pattern recognition. On the other hand, the o1 model can consider several ways before coming up with a solution, just like a human problem solver might consider various approaches before choosing a course of action. This makes it far more dependable in domains like sophisticated mathematics and scientific research that demand logic and precision.

Furthermore, the o1 model is better at identifying errors and modifying its logic.

Without a self-correction mechanism, previous models could produce results that were both correct and compelling. A more sophisticated error-detection mechanism was developed by OpenAI with o1, enabling the model to go back and review its responses as necessary. The emphasis on practical applications in the o1 model is another significant distinction. The o1 model has been specifically built to address use cases that differ from the conversational tasks that characterized prior versions of ChatGPT. It can now be used by researchers to annotate large, complicated datasets, by physicists to help solve problems related to quantum optics, and by medical practitioners to analyze biological data more thoroughly.

These practical uses highlight the model's wider applicability and promise. The o1 model, which offers enhanced language generation as well as sophisticated cognitive capabilities that bring AI closer than ever to human-like reasoning, essentially signifies the next stage in the evolution of AI.

Overview of Neural Networks, Machine Learning, and Reasoning Capabilities, the Underlying Technology

The o1 model, which is based on neural networks and machine learning, is a significant development in AI technology. The model's fundamental method of operation is deep learning, which enables it to process enormous volumes of data and identify patterns within it. O1 is built on a transformer architecture, just like its forebears, which is especially skilled at processing sequential data, like text. Nevertheless, the o1 model differs from previous ChatGPT iterations in that it has been refined and improved with more advanced reasoning skills. This system's fundamental component is a neural network, more especially a multi-layered network that enables the model to replicate how the human brain processes information.

These layers are made up of networked nodes, often known as neurons, that collaborate to interpret incoming data and generate language or answers to challenging issues. In order to enable o1 to comprehend deeper, more intricate links between bits of information in addition to surface-level patterns in text, each layer of the network processes data at a different level of abstraction. OpenAI has made major improvements to the reasoning skills of the o1 model, enabling it to perform tasks that were previously outside its capabilities. Its capacity to perform multi-step reasoning, dissecting complicated problems into smaller components and addressing them gradually, is one of the main innovations. This is similar to how people solve problems by breaking complex jobs down into smaller, easier-to-manage parts.

Justification for the Model's Capacity to "Think" for Prolonged Amounts of Time Before Reacting

The o1 model's capacity to "think" for extended periods of time before responding is one of its most innovative characteristics. Earlier iterations of ChatGPT's model produced answers rapidly, frequently by recognizing patterns right away without doing a thorough investigation. This hampered the AI's capacity to address problems requiring deep cognitive processing or multi-step thinking, even though it was helpful for many other tasks. The o1 approach overcomes this constraint by letting the AI deliberate over an issue for a longer period of time before reacting, simulating a more human-like reasoning process. This is a major change from earlier models—the capacity to halt, think, and select amongst various options.

OpenAI has taught o1 to "think" more deeply about complicated issues, weighing several possible solutions before selecting the best one. This procedure is similar to how people typically tackle challenging tasks—considering multiple strategies before choosing the most effective one. The model can attain more accuracy and reliability by delaying problem analysis, particularly when handling complex scientific, mathematical, or technical difficulties.

Impact on Handling Difficult Mathematical and Scientific Problems

Because of its improved reasoning abilities, the o1 model is especially well-suited to solving challenging mathematical and scientific problems. Long-term thinking is essential in disciplines like biology, chemistry, and quantum physics where issues frequently call for multi-layered answers. For example, the o1 model can produce sophisticated mathematical formulas in quantum optics, a subject renowned for its intricacy and abstract nature, helping researchers solve issues requiring profound cognitive reasoning. The model's capacity to annotate large datasets has already shown how it can advance medical research in the field of healthcare.

Biological data can be very complex, especially in domains like genomics, necessitating in-depth examination and multidimensional pattern detection. By analyzing these datasets more quickly, the o1 model can help researchers make faster discoveries and more accurate conclusions. O1's capacity to manage real-time problem-solving in ways that resemble human cognition is one of the biggest innovations. It is capable of performing tasks in computational simulations or iterative scientific operations that call for continuous analysis and modification.

This skill can shorten the time it takes to complete research projects and lessen the mental strain on human researchers—who might otherwise need years to solve difficult problems by hand. In conclusion, the o1 model represents a technological leap that goes beyond straightforward advancements in language generation. What differentiates it from other AI models is its capacity for lengthy thinking, critical thought prior to responding, and analysis of complicated situations. This development offers a window into the potential applications of artificial intelligence (AI) in healthcare, scientific research, and mathematical problem solving.

Chapter 2: The Capabilities of o1 – A Game Changer

Intricate Reasoning and Solving of Problems

The extraordinary capacity of OpenAI's o1 model for complex thinking and problem-solving, which represents a substantial improvement over its predecessors, is one of its most notable aspects. In contrast to previous versions of ChatGPT, which were mainly intended for conversational tasks and generic information retrieval, o1 is built to handle significantly more complex problems. The model's capacity to replicate human-like mental processes, such as analyzing issues for prolonged periods of time, weighing several approaches, and synthesizing complex answers, is crucial to this evolution. The o1 model has proven to be exceptionally adept at complex problems in scientific domains such as mathematics, physics, and biology. For instance, o1 may produce complex mathematical formulas in the field of physics, especially in fields like quantum optics.

This task frequently calls for in-depth theoretical knowledge and careful reasoning. The model tackles difficulties gradually, dissecting intricate questions into smaller, manageable pieces, rather than just reiterating previously established facts. Because of this, it is a good fit for scientific research where iterative problem-solving and abstract reasoning are essential. In the same way, the model can handle complex datasets in biology, such those from cell sequencing. Pattern recognition over large information scales and multi-layered analysis are frequently needed when dealing with biological data. O1 can do these jobs more effectively thanks to its sophisticated reasoning capabilities, which provide insights and solutions that formerly took a lot of human labor and time.

When it comes to modeling biological systems or annotating massive genomic datasets, o1's degree of reasoning introduces new efficiencies to the field. In math competitions such as the International Mathematics Olympiad, where it solved more than 80% of the questions, o1 has demonstrated exceptional problem-solving skills. This is no easy task because the challenges frequently call for higher-order, creative thinking in addition to rote memorizing of formulas. These kinds of complex riddles are easily solved by the model because of its capacity for lengthy, step-by-step reasoning, which makes it an effective tool in both professional and educational mathematics contexts.

Practical Uses: Cancer Research, Quantum Optics, and Other Areas

O1's reasoning powers have a plethora of real-world applications that could change numerous industries. Quantum optics, which studies how light behaves and interacts with matter at the quantum scale, is one of the most exciting fields. Problems in quantum optics are notoriously hard; they frequently need complicated mathematical computations that are difficult for even experienced researchers to complete. These sophisticated calculations, which the o1 model has proven capable of producing, could help physicists solve puzzles that may eventually lead to breakthroughs in industries like quantum computing and telecommunications. Research on cancer is another area where o1's aptitude for problem-solving is evident.

Large volumes of biological data, from patient health records to information from cell sequencing, are used in modern cancer research. It used to take a lot of time and human resources to process and interpret this data. But o1 is fast at analyzing these statistics, finding correlations and trends that human researchers might miss. In the field of genomics, for example, the model has the ability to annotate sizable DNA sequences, facilitating the understanding of genetic alterations and their connections to the development of cancer.

In doing so, o1 speeds up the process of discovery and makes it possible for more focused research to be conducted, which may result in advances in customized medicine and cancer treatments. Furthermore, by resolving intricate equations and simulating processes, o1 can help in the creation of novel chemical compounds in disciplines like chemistry. This is especially important for drug discovery, as it helps speed up the creation of novel medications by predicting the interactions between various compounds. Because of its sophisticated reasoning, the model can perform multi-step simulations and provide chemists with insights that would take months or even years to generate by hand. Beyond scientific fields, o1's potential is shown in engineering, finance, and environmental science, where complex problem-solving and modeling can be accomplished by utilizing its reasoning powers.

The o1 model is a revolutionary advancement in the field of artificial intelligence, capable of simulating the effects of climate change and forecasting market patterns based on massive datasets. It is at the vanguard of AI innovation due to its sophisticated reasoning and problem-solving abilities, which have the ability to completely change how we approach and tackle the most difficult problems of our day.

The Function of AI in Research and Healthcare

AI's Place in Research and Healthcare The development of AI has greatly improved our capacity to interpret complicated biological data and advance medicine. This is especially true with models like OpenAI's o1. Every day, the domains of biomedical research and healthcare produce enormous volumes of data, ranging from genetic sequences and patient records to imaging and epidemiological statistics. AI models like o1 are quickly becoming essential resources for this kind of data analysis, pattern recognition, and insight generation that can propel medical research.

An important function of o1 is to annotate complex biological data. For example, in the field of genomics, scientists are required to examine DNA sequences in order to comprehend genetic variants associated with diseases like cancer, diabetes, and cardiovascular disorders. The procedure of manually annotating these sequences takes a lot of effort and specialized knowledge. By automating this procedure with o1, scientists may use the reasoning powers of the model to find genetic markers and highlight mutations that warrant additional investigation. This not only expedites research but also lowers the possibility of human error, enabling more accurate and thorough analysis.

Additionally, medical image analysis is a crucial field of healthcare research that can benefit from the use of AI models like o1. For example, the interpretation of medical pictures from CT and MRI scans is crucial to the field of radiology. With an accuracy rate comparable to that of human radiologists, the o1 model can assess these images at a degree of detail that allows it to identify abnormalities like tumors or lesions. By supporting early disease diagnosis and expediting the diagnostic procedure, this enhances patient outcomes.

Applications of AI in Healthcare Research: Real-World Case Studies

The application of AI models to forecast the development of infectious illnesses is one noteworthy example study. AI was essential in the early stages of the COVID-19 pandemic, helping to forecast the virus's spread, analyze patient data, and even aid in the creation of vaccinations. By processing global epidemiological data, AI models were able to identify hotspots, possible mutations, and the pace of transmission, which enabled public health professionals to make well-informed judgments. With its sophisticated reasoning abilities, the o1 model can handle bigger information and make predictions that are more accurate, therefore supporting these kinds of endeavors. The search for new drugs is another use.

The enormous task of creating new medications, which requires evaluating millions of molecules in search of potent cures, is faced by pharmaceutical companies. The time and expense involved with using conventional drug development techniques are greatly decreased by the o1 model, which can simulate chemical reactions and forecast the effectiveness of therapeutic molecules. The model might be used, for instance, to forecast the interactions between particular medications and particular cancer cells, resulting in more specialized treatments. Models like o1 will become increasingly important in healthcare and research as AI develops because they provide faster, more accurate, and data-driven insights that have the potential to completely transform medicine.

Mathematics and Coding: Beyond Human Capacity?

In the domains of coding and mathematical problem-solving, where intricate and abstract problems frequently need enormous cognitive effort and knowledge, OpenAI's o1 model represents a substantial breakthrough. Humans have historically been the main forces behind innovation in many fields, relying on their aptitude for reason, imagination, and methodical problem-solving. But because to the development of AI models like o1, machines can now solve issues that were previously only regarded to be the purview of human expertise.

The Function of the o1 Model in Producing Coding Solutions and Complex Mathematical Formulas

The o1 model's extraordinary speed and accuracy in producing complex mathematical formulas is one of its main features. Complex multi-step calculations are frequently needed to solve mathematical issues in domains like quantum physics, fluid dynamics, and cryptography. O1 can solve these problems in a fraction of the time it would take human specialists days or even weeks to solve.

For instance, o1 can produce formulas that aid in the description of photon behavior at a quantum level when working on quantum optics difficulties, freeing up scientists to concentrate on research and practical applications rather than tedious computations. When it comes to coding, o1 is capable of handling complex software engineering problems in addition to basic programming assignments. The concept is perfect for automating repetitive coding jobs or debugging since it may develop efficient code by identifying patterns in current methods. More importantly, it can also provide creative fixes for coding issues, recommending fresh approaches to data processing or algorithm optimization that human developers might not have thought of. Because of this feature, o1 is a useful tool for fields including cybersecurity, data research, and software development.

How Accuracy and Efficiency Compare to Human Capabilities

The o1 model performs better than human skills in a number of critical areas when it comes to accuracy and efficiency. First, because it can "think" through an issue for prolonged periods of time without growing tired, it may methodically consider a number of possible answers before settling on the most accurate one. This makes it possible to generate formulas with almost flawless precision in mathematics, which lowers the possibility of human error caused by mental exhaustion or oversight.

Furthermore, o1 can process significantly larger datasets than a human programmer or mathematician could feasibly handle, which enables faster and more thorough problem-solving.

Though the model is incredibly efficient, it is important to remember that human intuition, creativity, and the capacity to approach issues in novel ways are still quite vital. These strengths are complemented by the o1 model, which provides creative pattern identification and fast computational support. However, human monitoring and interpretation are still required to guarantee that solutions are pertinent and useful in real-world situations. To sum up, the o1 model is a potent tool for math and coding that provides unmatched speed and precision when working on challenging assignments. It is a vital collaborator that pushes the frontiers of what is feasible in these domains, even though it might not be able to completely replace human expertise.

Chapter 3: Powering the AI – Energy Demands and Environmental Costs

The Unexpected Costs of AI's "Thinking"

The energy requirements of AI processing have become a major problem as AI continues to improve, especially with innovations like OpenAI's o1 model. The increased reasoning ability of the o1 model sets it apart from its predecessors and enables it to evaluate and solve complicated issues more efficiently. The increased energy expense of this improved capabilities, however, raises concerns about the long-term viability of widespread AI adoption. The extended reasoning process of the o1 model necessitates complex computations with large computing power requirements.

The model requires a significant amount of processing time for each "thinking" through of an issue, which results in increased energy use. Compared to conventional AI models that use quicker, less comprehensive reasoning patterns, this improvement can be orders of magnitude larger. It is not just marginal, though. For example, ChatGPT's o1 model may take seconds or even minutes to reach a conclusion, generating responses nearly instantly in the past, greatly increasing the power consumption of data centers housing such AI systems. The infrastructure needed to support these sophisticated models must also be taken into account when calculating energy.

Excessive quantities of electricity are required to run sophisticated algorithms on high-performance GPUs and TPUs. The need for more powerful hardware will rise along with the demand for AI services, which will result in an exponential rise in energy consumption. As a result, enterprises using the o1 model need to account for both the rising energy costs associated with the AI's increased capabilities and the operational costs of maintaining the system. #### **The Possible Cost to the Environment and Energy Infrastructure Issues Raised by Wide-Scale AI Implementation** AI's rising energy usage has important environmental consequences.

The increasing prevalence of AI systems such as o1 leads to an increased need for energy, which is primarily derived from fossil resources. Our dependence on it may make the environmental problems we face—such as resource depletion and climate change—worse. Data centers are well known for having large carbon footprints, and if energy sources do not switch to more sustainable options, the impact of AI technology could get worse. Furthermore, there are a variety of obstacles to energy infrastructure that arise from the widespread use of AI. The grid cannot support the additional load resulting from AI-driven processes in many places.

The integration of AI technologies across multiple sectors may be delayed as a result of the significant time and financial commitment required to upgrade the current infrastructure to meet this demand. Furthermore, when demand increases, energy prices will probably go up as well, which might have negative financial effects on companies that rely significantly on AI. Energy efficiency and sustainability must be given top priority in the AI community in order to allay these environmental worries. Some of the energy loads can be lessened by innovations in hardware design, such as creating processors that are more energy-efficient and optimizing algorithms that use less computing overhead.

In addition, lowering the carbon impact of using AI models requires switching to renewable energy sources like solar or wind power. In conclusion, even while the o1 model marks a major advancement in AI capabilities, it also comes with a high energy requirement and environmental consequences. To ensure that the advantages of sophisticated AI do not come at an unaffordable cost, researchers, legislators, and business leaders must work together to address these issues.

Harmonizing Sustainability and Innovation

It is critical to address the environmental impact of powerful AI models like OpenAI's o1, as their development and application grow more widespread. A multifaceted strategy that takes into account energy efficiency, technical improvements, and a dedication to lowering the carbon footprint associated with AI operations is needed to strike a balance between innovation and sustainability. Improving data centers' energy efficiency is among the best ways to lessen the effects of AI on the environment. Organizations can dramatically lower the amount of energy used during AI processing by making investments in state-of-the-art cooling solutions and more energy-efficient hardware. For instance, using liquid cooling systems can result in lower energy expenditures and carbon emissions since they can be far more efficient than conventional air cooling. Further reducing power usage is the switch to energy-efficient GPUs and TPUs made especially for AI applications.

Optimizing algorithms is another tactic to lower the processing demands of AI models. Similar performance levels can be achieved with reduced computer cost by streamlining complicated AI processes using techniques like model pruning, quantization, and knowledge distillation. This not only saves energy but also makes it possible to use AI in settings with limited resources. Organizations might also concentrate on powering their data centers using renewable energy sources. Businesses can significantly reduce their carbon footprints and encourage a more sustainable approach to AI development by making investments in solar, wind, or hydroelectric power.

A few of the biggest tech companies have already made the commitment to run their businesses entirely on renewable energy in order to become carbon neutral. Positively, partnerships between tech firms and energy suppliers can result in creative solutions, including the creation of green energy procurement contracts. In addition, it is critical to cultivate a sustainable culture within the AI community. Energy use can be greatly decreased by pushing scientists and developers to give environmental considerations top priority while creating and honing AI models. Campaigns for education and awareness can also emphasize the significance of sustainability, encouraging ethical AI development that is in line with international environmental objectives.

Government Policies and Business Reactions to Advanced AI's Energy Requirements

Government rules have a significant impact on how the AI sector responds to environmental issues and energy demands. Lawmakers have the chance to create frameworks that encourage environmentally friendly behavior while holding businesses responsible for their effects on the environment. Stricter energy efficiency regulations for data centers, for example, may incentivize businesses to spend more on environmentally friendly technology. The transition to more environmentally friendly AI operations may be accelerated by tax credits or grants for businesses that use renewable energy sources. Governments should encourage public-private collaborations in addition to legislative measures to encourage research in energy-efficient AI technologies. Research projects that involve collaboration can result in improvements in algorithm efficiency and hardware design, which in turn can lead to more sustainable AI practices.

Governments might also fund technology-related education and training initiatives that prepare workers to approach these issues with consideration. Although there has been a mixed response from the industry to the energy demands of advanced AI, there is a growing trend towards sustainability. Prominent technology corporations are starting to realize how critical it is to reduce their carbon footprints. Many have made commitments to challenging sustainability targets, such as committing to run operations entirely on renewable energy or reaching net-zero emissions by a particular year.

Additionally, in order to track and openly explain their environmental consequences, corporations are implementing sustainability reporting frameworks at an increasing rate. Moreover, industrial alliances are emerging to address the environmental issues that AI presents jointly. Through these partnerships, businesses can exchange resources, research, and best practices in order to foster sustainable innovation. Industry participants can present a united front by banding together to support environmentally conscious laws and guidelines that control the advancement of AI.

Industry participants and governmental organizations must work strategically to strike a balance between innovation and sustainability in the AI field. By placing a high priority on energy efficiency, making investments in renewable resources, and encouraging teamwork, the AI community may set the stage for a time when technical progress is in line with environmental responsibility.

Chapter 4: The Advantages of Human-like AI

Transforming Sectors: Education, Healthcare, and Other

The advent of AI models that mimic human behavior, such OpenAI's o1, has caused a paradigm shift in a number of businesses. These models have the potential to completely transform industries like healthcare, education, and the creative sector by improving efficiency, precision, and personalization in ways that were previously unthinkable. They do this by processing enormous amounts of data and possessing sophisticated reasoning abilities. The o1 model has the potential to greatly enhance patient care and diagnosis in the medical field. In the past, diagnosing complicated medical diseases has required a lot of work and frequently depended on the expert judgment of healthcare providers.

However, more precise and prompt diagnoses are made possible by o1's capacity to evaluate patient data, including medical history, test findings, and imaging. Artificial intelligence (AI) has the potential to discover patterns in tumor images that a human eye could overlook in oncology. This could result in early cancer detection and better treatment outcomes. Additionally, by incorporating AI into electronic health records, medical professionals can gain access to thorough insights that enable them to customize treatment regimens to meet the needs of specific patients, resulting in a more individualized approach to care.

By offering individualized learning experiences, the o1 model has the potential to revolutionize the way students learn in the field of education. The many learning demands of pupils are frequently ignored by traditional educational paradigms, which results in low interest and unsatisfactory performance. Using o1, teachers may make use of AI-powered tools that adjust to the unique learning preferences, styles, and rates of each student. The model may, for instance, evaluate how well a student does on tests and assignments, pinpointing their weak points and offering specialized help to fill them in. By making education more entertaining, this tailored attention not only improves comprehension but also cultivates a passion for learning.

Furthermore, the o1 model might function as a collaborator rather than a rival in the creative industries. AI can help with idea generation, music composition, and scriptwriting, for example, in media production. AI-generated recommendations can serve as a source of inspiration for musicians and filmmakers, hence expediting the creative process. Writers can now pursue new creative directions because AI can already provide engaging conversation and stories, as proven by companies like OpenAI. AI frees artists from routine work so they can concentrate on higher-order thinking and artistic expression, which eventually improves the cultural environment. Examples of these applications in the real world demonstrate the o1 model's revolutionary power.

In radiology departments, for example, AI-driven diagnostic technologies have already been implemented to help radiologists interpret medical pictures more reliably. AI is being used in education by platforms such as Khan Academy to tailor learning paths, which has a substantial positive impact on student engagement and results. AI has the potential to inspire designers and artists in the creative industry, as demonstrated by tools like DALL-E, which creates pictures based on text prompts. In conclusion, the o1 model has enormous potential to transform sectors including healthcare, education, and the arts. Organizations may improve diagnosis, tailor learning, and encourage innovation by utilizing its sophisticated capabilities, which will ultimately improve outcomes and enrich experiences for both individuals and society as a whole.

Enhancing Intelligence in Humans

The development of AI that can mimic human intelligence, especially with models like OpenAI's o1, offers a huge chance to enhance human intelligence across a range of fields. o1 fosters a cooperative interaction between humans and AI by improving problem-solving, creativity, and decision-making skills rather than taking the place of human abilities. This combination has enormous potential to transform how people approach problems and use their skills in the workforce of the future. O1 primarily improves human problem-solving through the provision of data-driven insights that guide decision-making procedures.

For human analysts, the sheer amount of data in many businesses can be daunting. The o1 model is capable of sorting through enormous datasets, spotting patterns, and clearly and concisely presenting relevant findings. Analysts in the finance industry, for instance, might use o1 to analyze risks, predict future trends, and assess market conditions. Professionals can make better decisions and decrease the chance of errors by incorporating AI into their decision-making toolkit. When it comes to creativity, o1 is a potent collaborator that lets people experiment with novel ideas and notions.

The model's capacity to produce original content can be exploited by writers, artists, and designers as a source of inspiration. This partnership may result in creative endeavors that combine human intuition with AI-generated concepts to produce original literary and artistic masterpieces. AI can be used by authors to generate story points or create character backstories, for example, or by musicians to work with AI to create new tunes and harmonies. o1 enables people to push the limits of their imagination and venture into unexplored territory by offering a creative partner. Beyond specific tasks, AI and human workers have the capacity to collaborate on larger organizational dynamics. AI models like o1 will improve team performance and productivity as they are more widely used in the workplace.

AI, for instance, can help teams in project management by monitoring progress, spotting bottlenecks, and making recommendations for changes. This makes the work environment more productive and collaborative by freeing up human workers to concentrate on strategic planning and the interpersonal components of project execution. However, a change in culture will be necessary for the effective integration of AI into the workforce. Companies need to adopt an attitude that views AI as an improvement tool rather than as a threat to jobs. This entails teaching staff members how to use AI tools efficiently and encouraging interdisciplinary cooperation between technologists and subject matter experts.

Organizations may fully utilize both human and AI strengths by cultivating an environment that does so. To sum up, the o1 model is a potent tool for boosting human intelligence and improving creativity, problem-solving, and decision-making in a variety of contexts. We can build a world where people are empowered to take on difficult tasks and develop in ways that were previously unthinkable by encouraging human-AI collaboration. Individuals gain from this synergy, which also propels growth across industries and, eventually, advances society.

Chapter 5: The Ethical Dilemma – A Machine That Thinks

Human-Like AI's Ethical Implications

The development of AI that can mimic human behavior, especially models like OpenAI's o1, raises important ethical issues that go against conventional wisdom about AI. The distinction between human and machine decision-making is becoming more and more hazy as AI systems show signs of being able to reason like humans. Important considerations concerning the nature of autonomy, accountability, and the moral frameworks required to direct the application of such technologies are brought up by this development. The idea of autonomy is among the most important ethical issues pertaining to AI that resembles humans. AI models may make judgments that have a big influence on people's lives as they develop sophisticated thinking abilities.

An AI system might, for example, suggest treatments in the healthcare industry based on large datasets and prediction algorithms. Although this can improve the results of medical treatments, it also begs the question of whose decisions those are. Who should bear the responsibility if an AI system makes a mistake in its recommendation—the AI, the healthcare providers, or the developers? A precise framework for assigning responsibility is necessary since the ethical landscape is complicated by the ambiguity around accountability. AI decision-making's potential for prejudice is a further ethical worry. Since AI systems are taught on historical data, they may be biased by society norms at the moment.

AI has the potential to reinforce or even worsen existing biases in crucial fields like financing, hiring, and law enforcement if it is not properly controlled. Biased decision-making can have disastrous consequences, especially for underprivileged populations whose decisions may lead to discrimination. Robust procedures for openness, supervision, and ongoing assessment of AI systems are necessary to address these biases and guarantee justice and equitable in their uses. Furthermore, when AI systems assume responsibilities that require human contact and decision-making, the consent debate gets more complicated. AI may interact with people in mental health applications, for instance, in a way that resembles human empathy and understanding.

The nature of these contacts and whether or not people are completely aware that they are interacting with a computer are ethical issues that are brought up by this. Consent must be carefully considered in light of the possibility of manipulation or emotional dependence on AI systems. This will help to ensure that users are empowered and educated when interacting with technology. Moreover, as AI systems grow increasingly independent, the moral ramifications of their decisions may reach previously uncharted territory for human agency. The use of AI in military applications, for instance, presents serious ethical issues. The distinction between human and machine decision-making may become more hazy if autonomous weapons with the power to make life-or-death decisions undermine conventional ideas of warfare and accountability.

This calls for a reconsideration of the moral standards that guide combat as well as the accountability of those who develop and use these technologies. In conclusion, there are many and complicated ethical ramifications for AI that resembles humans, including questions of accountability, autonomy, bias, and consent. As artificial intelligence (AI) systems advance, we must create strong ethical frameworks to direct their creation and application. Navigating this new environment and ensuring that the benefits of AI are harnessed responsibly and ethically requires interdisciplinary interaction among ethicists, engineers, policymakers, and society at large.

AI's Effect on Employment and Society

There are serious worries about how powerful AI systems, like OpenAI's o1, may affect employment and society at large as they become more and more integrated into different industries. Even while there is a lot of room for improvement in terms of efficiency and creativity, it is important to examine the risks associated with job displacement and social unrest. It is crucial to comprehend these processes in order to get ready for an increasingly AI-shaped future. The possibility of job displacement in a number of industries is among the most pressing worries.

There is a real concern that many jobs may become obsolete as AI systems become capable of carrying out tasks that have historically been performed by people, especially in roles involving repetitive or data-driven activity. AI-powered robotics, for example, can do jobs in manufacturing significantly more quickly and precisely than humans are capable of. Similarly, AI chatbots and virtual assistants are increasingly managing questions and providing support in industries like customer service, potentially decreasing the need for human agents. Different industries will experience different effects from AI on the labor market, but low-skilled jobs will be most vulnerable.

Employees in industries such as retail, administrative support, and transportation may be particularly susceptible to automation. The shift may not be smooth, despite some claims that AI would lead to new employment prospects in technology and related industries. Initiatives aimed at reskilling and upskilling workers will be crucial in preparing them for new tasks that arise as AI develops. The incorporation of artificial intelligence (AI) into daily life has wider social ramifications in addition to obvious economic ones. Economic inequality could rise as a result of job relocation. People who are unable to adjust to new occupations can experience financial instability, which could exacerbate social tensions.

Furthermore, communities that are highly dependent on particular industries may undergo considerable disruptions, leading to demands for focused policy interventions to assist the impacted parties. AI's socioeconomic ramifications also affect cultural dynamics. There may be changes in how people view human roles and value in society when AI systems make more and more decisions that have an impact on human lives. Concerns about the social contracts that regulate employment and the intrinsic value of human labor surface as computers take on tasks that were previously performed by people. Broader conversations regarding the purpose of employment and the social institutions that enable it may result from this.

To tackle these issues, governments, organizations, and society at large must take the initiative. Lawmakers must create structures, such as extensive retraining programs and social safety nets, to enable a fair transition for workers displaced by AI. Furthermore, promoting cooperation between academic institutions and business can assist in coordinating skill development with the changing needs of the labor market. In summary, the effects of AI on employment and society present a complex issue that needs serious thought. Although there is no denying the advantages of AI development, it is also important to consider the possibility of job loss and social unrest. Society can maximize the benefits of AI while reducing its negative consequences by proactively addressing these problems and giving equitable solutions first priority. This will ensure that technology will eventually augment human abilities rather than replace them.

The Dangers of AI Strengthening Social Inequalities and Preserving Biases

The introduction of AI systems into several facets of society gives rise to serious questions about inequality and prejudice. When AI models, such as OpenAI's o1, are used in decision-making procedures, the biases included in the training data are transferred to the model. Unintended effects may result from this, especially in delicate areas like recruiting, law enforcement, and healthcare, which could further entrench already-existing societal disparities. AI systems are trained using historical records that frequently depict prejudices, inequality, and social conventions.

An AI model might learn to prefer candidates that fit a particular profile, for example, if it is trained on hiring data from a corporation that has historically favored certain demographics. This might effectively exclude equally talented people from underrepresented groups. In addition to limiting these people's possibilities, this perpetuates systemic biases and makes it challenging to attain real equity in hiring practices. Biased algorithms in law enforcement can make racial profiling problems worse. AI programs that examine crime data may unfairly target underprivileged groups, which could result in over policing and unfair legal consequences. These applications demonstrate how crucial it is to carefully examine the datasets used in the training of AI algorithms and how urgently transparency in these algorithms is needed.

Furthermore, biased AI has an impact on society norms and perceptions in addition to specific circumstances. Biased AI systems have the potential to promote unfavorable stereotypes and affect public perception and behavior if they routinely produce skewed results. Because AI models continue to learn from biased data, this loop of bias has the potential to continue, exacerbating rather than lessening societal disparities. Organizations need to put strict auditing and validation procedures in place for AI systems in order to mitigate these dangers. To guarantee that a variety of viewpoints and experiences are taken into account, diverse teams should be included in the creation and management of AI technology. Furthermore, encouraging cooperation between social scientists and AI developers can aid in locating and reducing biases in algorithms and data.

Apprehensions Regarding AI's Use in Collecting and Abusing Personal Data

The risk of personal data being misused increases as AI technologies advance. The ability of models such as o1 to evaluate large volumes of data raises moral concerns over data security and privacy. AI systems are being used in a number of industries, such as marketing, healthcare, and law enforcement. As a result, there are a lot of hazards associated with the gathering and processing of personal data. The lack of transparency regarding data collection procedures is one of the main causes for concern. People frequently give out their personal information inadvertently when interacting online, but they might not completely comprehend how or by whom this information is used. Sensitive information like one's income, health, and personal preferences may be included in this data. This data could be utilized for eavesdropping or profit if there aren't strong rules and control in place.

The compilation of personal information may result in the development of thorough profiles that subject people to different types of abuse. For instance, consumer behavior can be manipulated by targeted advertising based on AI-generated profiles, which may influence people to make decisions that are not always in their best interests. In the medical field, improper use of personal information may result in prejudice when it comes to insurance coverage or available treatments. The possibility of privacy violations also prompts security worries. Malicious actors' techniques to take advantage of weaknesses in AI systems are becoming increasingly complex along with the systems themselves.

Cyberattacks directed against AI systems may expose private information, with dire repercussions for both people and businesses. Clear laws regulating data privacy and usage must be established with great effort in order to protect personal data. Governments, business executives, and civil society organizations need to work together to create comprehensive frameworks that put the rights of the individual first. Organizations should also implement ethical standards for gathering data, making sure that people are aware of the uses of their data and have choices for giving consent.

Talks Regarding How AI Should Be Managed and Regulated to Guarantee Safe Use

The increasing penetration of AI technology across many sectors underscores the criticality of establishing efficient governance and control procedures. A strong legislative framework is required to guarantee that these technologies are developed and applied in an ethical, transparent, and accountable manner given the speed at which models like o1 are progressing. The establishment of precise guidelines for development and implementation is a crucial component of AI governance. Best practices for data gathering, algorithm openness, and accountability need to be outlined by regulatory organizations. To address the complex issues raised by AI, these standards should be based on interdisciplinary viewpoints and include knowledge from ethicists, technologists, and social scientists.

The importance of supervision in the advancement of AI cannot be emphasized. It is crucial to conduct independent audits of AI systems in order to find biases, mistakes, and unexpected outcomes. Frequent evaluations can guarantee that AI models function impartially and openly, giving stakeholders trust in their use. Involving the public is also essential to forming AI governance. A more inclusive approach to regulation can be fostered by including a variety of viewpoints in talks regarding AI policy. Involving communities that AI systems may disproportionately affect and making sure their concerns are acknowledged and taken seriously are part of this. Given the global nature of AI development, international cooperation is required. Global guidelines for AI governance and ethics can be established to help reduce the hazards brought on by inconsistent enforcement of laws and cross-border data transfers.

Cooperation can also help countries learn from each other's experiences in AI governance by facilitating the sharing of knowledge. In conclusion, efficient governance and oversight over AI technologies are critical to guaranteeing their responsible and moral application. We can successfully negotiate the complex terrain of artificial intelligence (AI) while preserving individual rights and advancing societal well-being by establishing clear rules, encouraging independent scrutiny, including the public, and fostering international collaboration.

Chapter 6: The Potential Threat – Could o1 Outthink Humanity?

Superintelligence: A Fear

The creation of models like OpenAI's o1 has sparked discussions about the possibility of superintelligence, or intelligence beyond human cognitive capacities, as AI technology develops. This worry is not only theoretical; it represents anxieties based on practical and philosophical worries about how people and robots will interact in the future. Superintelligence poses serious concerns regarding safety, control, and the fundamentals of human decision-making. The idea that an artificial intelligence (AI) model, endowed with sophisticated reasoning and problem-solving skills, could surpass human intelligence in a variety of fields is the fundamental source of the concern surrounding superintelligence.

Even though o1 exhibits extraordinary aptitude in subjects like physics, math, and sophisticated decision-making, there is worry that its ability to learn and adapt could eventually cause it to create plans and solutions that are incomprehensible or uncontrollable to humans. We might be in uncharted ground if AI systems develop the ability to think independently at superintelligent levels. In this scenario, robots would dictate results based on logic that people are ill-equipped to question. Hypothetical situations where superintelligent AI acts with goals at odds with human ideals exacerbate this anxiety. For example, when an AI is assigned to solve a complicated global problem, such as resource allocation or climate change, it can use effective yet unethical or counterproductive techniques. In a situation like this, the possibility of a "utility maximization" strategy emerges, in which the AI ranks results solely on the basis of data and computations, possibly at the expense of people's lives or the wellbeing of society.

The terrifying ramifications of this are examined in a number of dystopian stories, where the cold, calculating nature of AI causes terrible outcomes. Moreover, the idea of a "intelligence explosion," in which an AI quickly advances its own powers beyond human control, is also a cause for concern regarding superintelligence. In this scenario, an AI may engage in recursive self-improvement, continuously and rapidly improving its abilities, once it reaches a certain degree of intelligence. As artificial intelligence develops into a type of intellect that functions without the input or limitations of humans, this could make human oversight unnecessary. The possibility of such a result presents moral conundrums about the boundaries of AI advancement and researchers' obligations to make sure that these technologies continue to be consistent with human values. Furthermore, there are more vulnerabilities in the infrastructure itself that underpins AI, including the enormous data centers that run these systems.

A superintelligent AI could take advantage of flaws in the environment in which it operates and manipulate systems to accomplish its goals. This could result in situations where AI not only outperforms humans in intelligence but also actively works to subvert human authority, posing a confrontation between humans and the very instruments they designed. It is crucial that developers, legislators, and ethicists have proactive conversations about the future of AI in order to reduce these hazards. Designing and using AI systems like o1 within moral bounds can be ensured by putting in place strict supervision procedures, establishing safety guidelines, and encouraging interdisciplinary cooperation.

Having public discussions on the ramifications of superintelligence can help foster a more knowledgeable and circumspect attitude toward the advancement of AI. In conclusion, there is a great deal of dread around superintelligence, even if models such as o1 provide incredible prospects for progress. Because AI has the ability to outsmart humans, its ramifications must be carefully considered. This includes a focus on ethical issues, strong governance, and a dedication to ensuring AI stays a tool for human benefit rather than a source of existential threat.

Who Should Oversee the Creation and Application of Such Potent AI?

The swift progress of artificial intelligence technology, such as OpenAI's o1, prompts important inquiries on accountability, authority, and management. With the increasing sophistication of AI systems, supervision is essential. The question of who should be in charge of the creation and application of these potent technologies is complicated and involves social, legal, and ethical issues. First and foremost, it is critical to understand that multiple parties share accountability for overseeing AI. Rather, a multi-stakeholder strategy is required.

Governments, IT firms, educational institutions, and civil society organizations are all included in this. Governments are essential in creating the legal frameworks that guarantee the ethical and safe advancement of artificial intelligence. In order to do this, rules and regulations addressing topics like algorithmic transparency, data protection, and accountability for AI-driven judgments must be developed.

As the main corporations creating AI systems, technology companies also have a big part to play. In order to minimize prejudices and guarantee that their innovations serve the greater benefit of society, they must give ethical issues top priority during the design process and incorporate a variety of viewpoints. As part of this, impact evaluations are carried out to determine the possible outcomes of their AI systems prior to implementation. International organizations can also help nations collaborate and have discussions about AI governance. Because technology is a global phenomenon, cross-border issues like data sharing and the possibility of AI misuse require cooperation.

International frameworks and agreements can aid in harmonizing laws and make sure that the development of AI complies with common ethical norms. Public participation is yet another essential element of efficient governance. Including a range of perspectives in talks regarding AI regulations can improve openness and responsibility, which will increase public confidence in AI systems. Campaigns for education and awareness can enable people to comprehend the consequences of artificial intelligence and take part in determining its destiny. In conclusion, cooperation amongst a variety of stakeholders is necessary for the governance of strong AI systems like o1. Society can negotiate the intricacies of AI governance and guarantee that these technologies are produced and used responsibly by creating thorough regulatory frameworks, encouraging moral behavior within tech businesses, interacting with international authorities, and encouraging public involvement.

The Dangers of Using Cutting-Edge AI for Military Uses

There are a lot of hazards and moral conundrums associated with integrating AI technologies into military applications. The possibility of using sophisticated AI systems in combat raises concerns about the effects on international security, human rights, and the continuation of armed conflict as countries investigate the use of AI for defense. The creation of autonomous weapon systems that can function without direct human intervention is one of the most urgent issues. These devices, sometimes called "killer robots," are capable of using data analysis and algorithms to decide between life and death. The idea that robots will decide whether to launch an attack or attack a person is extremely unsettling because it takes people out of important judgments involving moral and ethical standards.

Lack of human judgment increases the possibility of mistakes, misidentifications, and unexpected outcomes, which can result in the death of innocent people and intensification of hostilities. Furthermore, if AI is used in combat, countries may engage in an arms race to surpass one another in terms of scientific advancement. International relations might become unstable and the likelihood of conflict would rise as a result of this competitiveness leading to the rapid development of autonomous weapon systems without sufficient regulatory control. The possibility of disastrous outcomes increases when nations make large investments in AI-driven military technologies, particularly if such systems end up in the hands of non-state actors or rogue states. Deeply held ethical questions surround the use of AI in combat. It is a challenge to basic accountability and responsibility standards to entrust life-and-death choices to robots.

Determining responsibility gets hard in situations where an autonomous weapon system results in civilian casualties. It is unclear who is ultimately accountable—the machine's maker, the military people who used it, or both. Public confidence in military operations may be damaged by this ambiguity, which could result in a lack of responsibility. Moreover, it is impossible to ignore the psychological effects on both soldiers and society at large. AI in battle has the potential to normalize conflict by desensitizing people to violence and war. The distance between combatants and the repercussions of their actions could lessen the moral significance of decisions made in the heat of battle as warfare becomes more mechanized. In conclusion, there are a lot of risks associated with using AI in combat, which calls for regulation and cautious thought.

To avoid any abuses and guarantee that human oversight stays at the center of military decision-making, it is imperative to establish international rules and agreements to regulate the development and deployment of autonomous weapon systems. Humanity may prioritize ethical norms and safety while navigating the challenging terrain of AI in warfare by addressing these ethical concerns and putting strong protections in place.

Chapter 7: In Search of Balance – Integrating AI into Society Responsibly

A Novel Collaboration: AI and Humans

Society is at a critical turning point as AI technology, especially models such as OpenAI's o1, continues to advance and penetrate many facets of existence. The difficulty is figuring out how to live with AI that is becoming more and more like us while yet improving our abilities and upholding moral principles. It takes careful planning to approach this new alliance between humans and AI, with an emphasis on cooperation rather than rivalry. Redefining the roles of humans and AI is the first step in this cooperation.

AI should be welcomed by society as a tool that enhances human intelligence and productivity rather than being seen as a replacement for human labor. For instance, by evaluating large datasets, AI in healthcare can help physicians diagnose illnesses more precisely, freeing up staff members to concentrate on patient care and emotional support. This change in perspective has the potential to boost output and improve results in a number of industries. Establishing a collaborative culture is crucial to promoting harmonious coexistence. As part of this, multidisciplinary collaboration between AI experts, ethicists, and subject matter experts is encouraged in order to create AI applications that are both morally and practically sound. Transparency in AI development should be a top priority for organizations, enabling stakeholders to comprehend the underlying algorithms and decision-making procedures. By doing this, people and AI systems can develop trust, ensuring that these technologies are seen as allies rather than enemies.

In order to prepare society for this cooperation, education is essential. As artificial intelligence (AI) permeates more aspects of daily life, educational systems must adapt to provide students with the skills they need to succeed in an AI-enhanced world. Teaching data literacy, critical thinking, and ethical issues with AI use are all part of this. Through educating the next generation about the potential and constraints of artificial intelligence, society may produce knowledgeable individuals who can interact with these technologies in productive ways. Furthermore, it's critical to establish forums for public discussion on the ramifications of AI.

Talking about AI with communities can help people understand the technology and become more involved in its ethical governance. Promoting diversity in the development process guarantees that AI applications represent the demands and values of a wide range of society. In the end, putting ethical and human welfare concerns first is necessary to create ethical approaches to integrate AI. As AI develops, society has to make a commitment to make sure that these innovations fulfill rather than limit human potential. This collaboration has the potential to have revolutionary effects in a number of fields, paving the way for a time when AI and people will collaborate to solve difficult problems and enhance quality of life.

How Education Systems Must Change to Readiness Future Generations for an AI-Powered World

The school system needs to change as AI technologies proliferate in order to equip the next generation for a world where these tools will have a greater impact. This progression is essential for developing students' technical proficiency as well as their profound comprehension of the moral, societal, and financial ramifications of artificial intelligence. Education must promote transdisciplinary learning above all else. A curriculum that integrates computer science, ethics, social studies, and critical thinking should be taught to students. With this all-encompassing method, students will be able to comprehend artificial intelligence (AI) as a social force as well as a technological tool.

For example, bringing up the ethical implications of AI in history or social science classes can inspire students to think critically about the ways in which technology impacts people's lives and social institutions. Moreover, the curriculum ought to incorporate practical experience with AI technologies. Students' practical abilities can be improved by participating in coding seminars, using AI tools, and working on real-world problems using programs. These programs can also foster innovation and creativity, motivating students to use AI to create answers for urgent global issues. Teachers also need to stress the significance of lifelong learning. The abilities needed to traverse the world of AI will also advance as it develops. Even after graduation, educational institutions should encourage students to explore further learning opportunities in AI-related subjects by fostering a culture of ongoing education. In order to create easily available resources for upskilling, this may entail forming relationships with IT businesses, online learning platforms, and community organizations.

Policy Changes Needed to Effectively Regulate and Manage AI on a Global Level

To properly control and manage AI on a worldwide basis, considerable policy improvements are necessary in addition to educational reforms. Governments must set forth precise regulations governing the creation, application, and usage of AI. This entails developing thorough legal frameworks that cover matters like algorithmic accountability, data privacy, and moral AI practices. Setting guidelines for AI system openness is an important issue for policy attention. Businesses ought to be compelled to reveal the data they use, the algorithms they employ, and any potential biases in their systems. Because of this transparency, consumers and regulators will be able to hold AI developers responsible and guarantee that technologies are used properly.

Furthermore, successful regulation of AI depends on international cooperation. Because technology is an international field, countries need to collaborate to develop best practices and common standards. This might entail the establishment of global organizations for AI governance, modeled after those already in place to regulate commerce or climate change. Countries can solve cross-border issues like data sharing and the possibility of AI technology misuse by working together on AI rules. Policies should also support the development of ethical AI research and technology. Governments have the authority to finance projects that give ethical issues top priority and to promote programs that include a variety of stakeholders in the AI development process. This will make it easier to guarantee that AI technology represents a variety of viewpoints and advance society.

Policy changes and educational reform must be implemented simultaneously to adequately prepare the next generation for life in an AI-powered environment. Education systems should change to prioritize interdisciplinary learning, practical experience, and lifelong learning so that people may acquire the skills necessary to succeed in an AI-enhanced future. In addition, strong legal frameworks and international collaboration will contribute to the responsible development and application of AI, paving the way for a time when AI and humans can live in harmony.

Chapter 8: The Future of AI – What Comes After o1?

OpenAI's Future Prospects

An important turning point in the development of artificial intelligence has been reached with the introduction of OpenAI's o1 model, which reflects both the quick pace of technological improvement and the lofty goals for the field's future. This model raises the bar for what artificial intelligence (AI) is capable of because of its improved reasoning abilities and capacity to solve challenging issues. The goal of OpenAI's vision goes beyond o1, with the goal of creating models that are capable of prolonged reasoning over the course of days or even weeks, radically altering the way we approach problem-solving and scientific research.

According to OpenAI, AI models will play a crucial role in research and innovation in the future. These models' capacity to "think" for extended periods of time offers a paradigm shift in the way we approach difficult problems in a variety of disciplines, such as environmental science, engineering, and healthcare. An AI model that can continuously evaluate and improve hypotheses over weeks, for example, might greatly speed up the development of new medicines in the drug discovery process. With the ability to handle large datasets and produce insights instantly, this kind of model would allow academics to investigate hitherto unexplored areas. Furthermore, this vision highlights how crucial human-AI collaboration is.

OpenAI aims to develop models that improve human creativity and critical thinking in addition to offering answers. As AI systems develop in strength, they will be able to assist researchers with new ideas, data pattern recognition, and experiment design. This mutually beneficial partnership will spur fresh research and creative thinking in addition to raising production. OpenAI's future vision places a strong emphasis on addressing the societal and ethical ramifications of developing AI. The group is dedicated to making sure that artificial intelligence (AI) technologies are created and used ethically, with an emphasis on accountability and openness. Robust governance mechanisms are important due to the increased potential for exploitation that comes with advanced models.

The goal of OpenAI is to collaborate with ethicists, legislators, and the general public to create standards that support the responsible and moral application of AI technologies. Future AI models should strive for more than just computational efficiency; they should also advance science and deepen our knowledge of complicated systems. For instance, the ability to simulate complex biological processes may result in advances in our knowledge of illnesses at the molecular level. Through long-term simulation of biological system interactions, scientists may be able to learn things that help develop new treatment approaches. Furthermore, OpenAI hopes to use these sophisticated models to address global issues like resource management and climate change.

Policies and programs targeted at sustainability may be influenced by AI systems that can evaluate environmental data and forecast long-term trends. Artificial Intelligence (AI) can help with strategic planning and informed decision-making for a more sustainable future by allowing scientists to conduct simulations across longer time spans. In conclusion, the o1 model serves as an example of OpenAI's ambitious and comprehensive vision for the future of AI. It includes advances in computational power as well as a dedication to moral improvement and the well of society. The potential for these models to transform research and tackle urgent global issues is becoming more and more apparent as AI develops. The course that o1 has established is only the start of a revolutionary voyage that will undoubtedly change science and technology for future generations.

Theories Regarding AI's Potential to Address the Biggest Issues Facing Humanity

Might AI Models of the Future Provide Answers to the World's Problems, Including Poverty and Climate Change? The promise of artificial intelligence (AI) to solve humanity's most urgent problems is both exciting and scary as we stand at the crossroads of technological growth. Subsequent artificial intelligence models, particularly those possessing improved cognitive and prognostic abilities, may be crucial in addressing pressing worldwide issues including poverty, healthcare inequalities, and climate change. Climate change is one of the most pressing issues facing humanity.

Large volumes of environmental data may be processed by advanced AI to forecast various climatic scenarios, assess the effects of human activity, and improve resource management. AI-driven models, for example, can determine the best ways to cut carbon emissions across a range of industries, including transportation and energy generation. AI has the potential to assist governments and organizations in making well-informed decisions about infrastructure expenditures and policy changes by forecasting future climate patterns. Furthermore, through forecasting energy use and optimizing energy supply from solar, wind, and other sources, AI can enhance the management of renewable energy.

Artificial Intelligence has the ability to boost economic growth and raise living standards in the area of poverty alleviation. To determine the underlying factors that contribute to poverty in certain areas, machine learning algorithms can evaluate socioeconomic data. AI can assist in maximizing resource allocation by customizing interventions based on regional needs, such as job training and education programs. AI-powered financial solutions can also help underprivileged populations obtain loans and financial services, which will encourage entrepreneurship and economic empowerment. Another important area where AI might have a big impact is healthcare.

Cutting-edge AI algorithms are able to customize treatment regimens for patients, forecast disease outbreaks, and evaluate medical data. AI can help with medication discovery and the creation of targeted medicines for illnesses like cancer by analyzing genomic data. Proactive health management and early intervention can result from the ability to combine and analyze data from several sources, including wearable devices, which can eventually improve patient outcomes. AI can also improve education by offering individualized learning programs that are catered to each student's needs. AI is able to create personalized curriculums that fill in knowledge gaps and increase student engagement by evaluating student performance and learning preferences. This strategy may aid in closing the gap in educational opportunities, giving students in environments with limited resources access to high-quality instruction.

There is a great deal of promise for future AI models to help solve the world's problems, including poverty and climate change. AI has the potential to significantly impact society advancement through the use of personalized interventions, predictive modeling, and sophisticated data analysis. However, to ensure that AI technologies are used for the greater good, fulfilling this promise requires a commitment to ethical development and cross-sector collaboration.

The Way Ahead: Prospects and Dangers

The Careful Balance Between Reducing Existential Risks and Using AI for Social Good As artificial intelligence develops, there are considerable hazards associated with the opportunities it offers.

The difficulty is striking a balance between the potential advantages of AI and the necessity to lessen existential risks that can result from improper use or unforeseen repercussions. It is imperative that we proceed cautiously, strategically, and with a dedication to responsible innovation. The possibility of unforeseen effects is one of the main worries with AI development. AI systems run the possibility of acting in ways that are inconsistent with human ideals as they get more independent.

For example, if an AI isn't closely watched, it may unintentionally make inequality worse by optimizing resource allocation. Developers must give ethical issues top priority when designing AI systems in order to mitigate these hazards. They must also make sure that these systems are accountable, transparent, and in line with society ideals. Furthermore, the use of AI in crucial fields like surveillance and national security raises moral concerns about civil liberties and privacy. Strong laws and control are required since AI-driven surveillance technologies have the potential to violate people's rights. To guard against misuse and guarantee that technologies advance the public good, policymakers must set forth precise rules controlling the application of AI in delicate fields. Automation's ability to eliminate jobs is a serious issue as well.

Many functions that are currently completed by humans may be automated as AI technologies advance, which could result in a widespread loss of jobs in several industries. Even though AI can increase efficiency and production, it is important to consider the social and economic effects of this change. To assist those impacted by automation, measures like social safety nets and retraining programs must be put in place. AI has a bright future ahead of it, despite these obstacles. Together, engineers, ethicists, legislators, and the general public can strive toward a time when artificial intelligence (AI) is used for positive purposes.

In order to do this, multidisciplinary study on the moral, societal, and financial implications of AI technology must be encouraged. It is imperative to make a conscious innovation call. Fairness, openness, and diversity should be the guiding values for AI development. It is possible to guarantee that technologies encompass a broad spectrum of viewpoints and values by involving a variety of stakeholders in the development and implementation of AI systems. In conclusion, there are hazards and opportunities associated with AI's future. We can use AI as a tool for good while protecting against existential risks if we prioritize ethical development, encourage cooperation, and address potential social effects. It is our collective duty as citizens, developers, and legislators to make sure that AI technologies support a fair, sustainable, and just future for all people.

Conclusion: A Machine Like Human – Friend or Foe?

Synopsis of AI's Social Impact The introduction of sophisticated AI models, such OpenAI's o1, marks a turning point in technological advancement with broad ramifications for society. These artificial intelligence systems have a plethora of potential benefits that span multiple domains, including healthcare and education, and address some of humanity's most critical issues. But this enormous potential comes with a lot of risks and moral conundrums that need to be carefully considered. The ability of AI models like o1 to process and analyze enormous volumes of data has had a significant impact on numerous fields, resulting in breakthroughs.

AI, for example, can help with disease diagnosis, treatment plan optimization, and medication discovery in the healthcare industry. Artificial intelligence (AI) has the potential to accelerate the development of novel treatments by sorting through intricate biological data and spotting trends. This has the potential to completely transform healthcare delivery, making it more efficient and individualized. Artificial Intelligence has the ability to revolutionize education.

Artificial Intelligence (AI) can assist close educational gaps and enhance results by providing customized curriculum based on each student's needs. This flexibility can encourage a more inclusive learning environment by enabling students to learn at their own speed. Furthermore, it's remarkable how AI is being used to address global problems like poverty and climate change. Artificial intelligence (AI) can assist policymakers in making well-informed decisions that support sustainability by evaluating environmental data and forecasting future events. In a similar vein, artificial intelligence (AI) can optimize resource distribution to fight poverty and make sure that aid reaches the right people. Even with these encouraging advantages, there are serious concerns about the use of advanced AI models.

An important ethical conundrum is the possibility of prejudice in AI decision-making. Inaccurate or non-representative training data for these models could cause the AI to reinforce already-existing societal disparities. Thus, it is essential to guarantee that AI systems are impartial, open, and responsible. The effect of AI on jobs is another urgent concern. Automating tasks that were previously completed by people has the potential to destabilize the economy and cause job displacement. Although AI has the potential to increase productivity, it is important to think about the social implications of these developments and put policies in place to support the impacted workforce. Furthermore, there is concern over the potential for malicious or inappropriate use of AI technology.

Artificial intelligence (AI) systems have the potential to be used for malicious purposes, such as cyberwarfare, spying, or even autonomous weaponry, as they get more self-sufficient. These scenarios demonstrate the necessity of strict laws and moral standards guiding the creation and application of AI. In conclusion, even while AI models like o1 have a lot of potential benefits, there are also a lot of risks and moral conundrums associated with them. It is difficult to strike a balance between utilizing AI for social good and reducing its hazards, thus developers, legislators, and society at large must take the initiative.

Human-Machine Collaboration's Future

The topic of how AI and humans will work together becomes more and more important as we move toward the future. Artificial intelligence (AI) has enormous potential to advance human capabilities, but responsible innovation and ethical considerations must guide its development.

Emphasizing the enhancement of human intelligence rather than its replacement is a crucial component of future human-machine collaboration. More sophisticated AI systems can manage monotonous jobs and intricate data analysis, freeing up humans to concentrate on higher-order cognitive functions like creativity and emotional intelligence.

AI, for instance, can work as a collaborative partner in creative industries like literature, music, and painting, providing ideas and inspiration while letting human artists keep control over the finished work. Furthermore, successful integration of AI across numerous domains will require interdisciplinary collaboration. This comprises not just developers and technologists, but also sociologists, ethicists, and members of the impacted communities. Incorporating a range of viewpoints during the development phase guarantees that artificial intelligence systems are created with a thorough comprehension of their societal consequences. This cooperative method can assist in detecting possible prejudices and moral dilemmas before they materialize in practical implementations.

To educate future generations for a society increasingly integrated with AI, education systems must adapt in addition to fostering multidisciplinary collaboration. Modifications to the curriculum that prioritize digital literacy, ethical reasoning, and critical thinking will provide students the tools they need to successfully negotiate the challenges of human-AI interaction. People can be empowered to use AI technology responsibly if we promote awareness of their potential and constraints. Furthermore, legislators have a significant influence on how AI is developed. It is imperative to establish comprehensive regulatory frameworks that give ethical considerations and public safety top priority. Regulations ought to cover matters like responsibility, transparency, and data privacy in AI systems.

We can make sure that these technologies serve the public interest by fostering an atmosphere that encourages ethical AI development. The future of cooperation between humans and machines ultimately depends on how both parties define progress. We can fully utilize AI as a tool for good by encouraging responsible innovation and giving ethical issues top priority. Rather than causing harm or division, the objective should be to establish a synergistic partnership where AI improves human talents and tackles urgent global concerns. In conclusion, even though there are many obstacles in our path, it is possible for AI to cohabit with humans in a way that is advantageous. We can traverse the complexity of AI and make sure that it continues to be a friend rather than a threat in our quest for a better future through cooperation, education, and responsible governance.

www.ingramcontent.com/pod-product-compliance
Lightning Source LLC
Chambersburg PA
CBHW071102240526
45471CB00016B/2304